20 Answers

Scripture & Tradition

Jim Blackburn

All booklets are published thanks to the generous support of the members of the Catholic Truth Society

CATHOLIC TRUTH SOCIETY
PUBLISHERS TO THE HOLY SEE

Originally published as 20 Answers: Scripture & Tradition. *© Copyright 2015 Catholic Answers, Inc. 2020 Gillespie Way, El Cajon, California 92020.*

ISBN 978 1 78469 110 3

Introduction

All Christians generally agree that Christian doctrine must be determined in accordance with God's revelation. It makes sense that everything God has revealed is worthy of belief and, in many cases, necessary for salvation. Indeed, Jesus, quoting from Deuteronomy 8:3, emphasises the importance of the *word of God*: "It is written, 'Man shall not live by bread alone, but by every word that proceeds from the mouth of God'" (*Mt* 4:4).

Tragically, though, not all Christians agree on what God's word is, and thus do not agree on all matters of Christian doctrine.

Most non-Catholic Christians claim that the Bible alone is the word of God. This is a relatively novel idea in the history of Christianity, having come to the fore only since the time of the Protestant Reformation. For most of Christian history, Christians have believed that Scripture does not constitute the entirety of the deposit of faith that the first Christians received long before a book of the New Testament was ever written (see *Jude* 3).

That faith was first delivered to the early Church orally, not in writing. Scholars nearly unanimously agree that the first books of the New Testament (1 and 2 Thessalonians) were not written until the middle of the first century, around AD 50-52. Yet, even without these books, the revelation of Jesus Christ was being spread through the oral teaching of the apostles and their successors. The books of the New Testament came to be written over a period of several decades, and it was not always immediately apparent exactly how they should be understood (see *2 P* 3:16). So the early Christians came to interpret them correctly through authoritative oral teaching - what the Church calls Sacred Tradition (see *2 P* 1:20-21).

Since the Protestant Reformers rejected Sacred Tradition, the descendants of their faith tradition have been left with only their own fallible interpretations of Scripture alone (*sola scriptura*) with which to determine their doctrines. This has resulted in countless disagreements and widespread splintering into thousands of Christian denominations.

It is my hope that this booklet will help to dispel the myth of *sola scriptura* and be a useful instrument for helping Christians fully embrace the word of God.

1. What is the "word of God"?

The term *word of God* refers to God's divine revelation to humanity, in which he reveals himself to us for the sake of our salvation. The Vatican II document *Dei Verbum* (*DV*) explains:

> Through divine revelation, God chose to show forth and communicate himself and the eternal decisions of his will regarding the salvation of men. That is to say, he chose to share with them those divine treasures which totally transcend the understanding of the human mind. (6)

Christians generally agree that the *fulness* of God's revelation is the Son of God, Jesus Christ. St John begins his Gospel writing about the "Word" in this sense:

> In the beginning was the Word, and the Word was with God, and the Word was God. He was in the beginning with God; all things were made through him, and without him was not anything made that was made. In him was life, and the life was the light of men. The light shines in the darkness, and the darkness has not overcome it. (*Jn* 1:1-5)

Word of God is used in this same sense elsewhere in the New Testament,[1] but we also find a secondary sense of the term: to refer to the spoken and written revelation of God upon which Christian teaching is based, and which is passed on from generation to generation. For example, in the Acts of the Apostles, Luke writes about "preaching the word of God" (6:2) and how it "increased" (6:7) as well as "grew and multiplied" (12:24). In Acts 13, the word of God is "proclaimed" (13:5), "spoken" (13:46), and people came to "hear" it (13:7, 44). In Acts 18, St Paul is depicted "teaching" the word of God (18:11).

It is this secondary sense of the term that Christians most often have in mind when we refer to the revelation of God that has been entrusted to the Church and taught throughout history. It contains the truths that Christians must believe and make active in our lives for the sake of our salvation and the salvation of others. St Jude calls it "the faith which was once for all delivered to the saints" (*Jude* 3).

Jesus entrusted this *deposit of faith* to the apostles and their successors, guided by the Holy Spirit, to be safeguarded from corruption and taught in every age just as Jesus commissioned them to do before his Ascension (see *Mt* 28:19-20).

Dei Verbum elaborates:

> In his gracious goodness, God has seen to it that what he had revealed for the salvation of all nations would abide perpetually in its full integrity and be handed on to all generations. Therefore Christ the Lord in whom the full revelation of the supreme God is brought to completion (see 2 *Co* 1:20; 3:13; 4:6), commissioned the apostles to preach to all men that gospel which is the source of all saving truth and moral teaching, and to impart to them heavenly gifts. This gospel had been promised in former times through the prophets, and Christ himself had fulfilled it and promulgated it with his lips. (7)

It is important to recognise that the apostles carried out their commission both through preaching *and* writing. The *Catechism of the Catholic Church* (*CCC*) explains:

In keeping with the Lord's command, the gospel was handed on in two ways:

1. *Orally* by the apostles who handed on, by the spoken word of their preaching, by the example they gave, by the institutions they established, what they themselves had received - whether from the lips of Christ, from his way of life and his works, or whether they had learned it at the prompting of the Holy Spirit.

2. *In writing* by those apostles and other men associated with the apostles who, under the inspiration of the same Holy Spirit, committed the message of salvation to writing (76).

In the Catholic Church, we refer to the apostles' preaching, examples, and institutions as *Sacred Tradition* (or *apostolic tradition*) and their writing (including the Old Testament that they received from the Jews) as *Sacred Scripture*. Many other Christians believe that only the written Bible is the word of God. They see Scripture alone as the only definitive source of divine truth. Catholics, however, believe that God did not limit his revelation to a book; instead he gave his saving truth to mankind in two complementary and equally authoritative forms.

> There exists a close connection and communication between Sacred Tradition and Sacred Scripture. For both of them, flowing from the same divine wellspring, in a certain way merge into a unity and tend toward the same end... [I]t is not from Sacred Scripture alone that the Church draws her certainty about everything which has been revealed. Therefore both Sacred Tradition and Sacred Scripture are to be accepted and venerated with the same sense of loyalty and reverence. (*DV* 9).

Thus, the Catholic Church bases its teaching upon one source: the word of God, transmitted to his people in two ways.

2. What is Sacred Scripture?

Sacred Scripture is the written form of the word of God. It comprises the books of the Old and New Testaments, that is, the Christian Bible.

The Old Testament is important because it sets the foundation for the fulness of God's revelation in Jesus Christ. *Dei Verbum* explains:

> The plan of salvation foretold by the sacred authors, recounted and explained by them, is found as the true word of God in the books of the Old Testament: these books, therefore, written under divine inspiration, remain permanently valuable. The principal purpose to which the plan of the old covenant was directed was to

> prepare for the coming of Christ, the redeemer of all and of the messianic kingdom, to announce this coming by prophecy (*Lk* 24:44; *Jn* 5:39; *1 P* 1:10), and to indicate its meaning through various types (*1 Co* 10:12). Now the books of the Old Testament, in accordance with the state of mankind before the time of salvation established by Christ, reveal to all men the knowledge of God and of man and the ways in which God, just and merciful, deals with men. These books, though they also contain some things which are incomplete and temporary, nevertheless show us true divine pedagogy. These same books, then, give expression to a lively sense of God, contain a store of sublime teachings about God, sound wisdom about human life, and a wonderful treasury of prayers, and in them the mystery of our salvation is present in a hidden way. Christians should receive them with reverence. (*DV* 14-15)

So the Old Testament remains a valuable part of God's word as it prepares the way for Christ. Yet it cannot be fully understood apart from the New Testament, in which the preparation comes to fruition. In the New Testament we find the fulfilment of the revelation of the Old. *Dei Verbum* continues:

> The word of God, which is the power of God for the salvation of all who believe (see *Rm* 1:16), is set forth and shows its power in a most excellent way in the

writings of the New Testament. For when the fulness of time arrived (*Ga* 4:4), the Word was made flesh and dwelt among us in his fulness of graces and truth (*Jn* 1:14). Christ established the kingdom of God on earth, manifested his Father and himself by deeds and words, and completed his work by his death, resurrection and glorious Ascension and by the sending of the Holy Spirit. Having been lifted up from the earth, he draws all men to himself (*Jn* 12:32), He who alone has the words of eternal life (see *Jn* 6:68). This mystery had not been manifested to other generations as it was now revealed to his holy apostles and prophets in the Holy Spirit (*Ep* 3:4-6), so that they might preach the Gospel, stir up faith in Jesus, Christ and Lord, and gather together the Church. Now the writings of the New Testament stand as a perpetual and divine witness to these realities. (*DV* 17)

Thus, the Old Testament and the New Testament together bring us the revelation of salvation history. The Old Testament prepares us for the New. The New Testament brings to light and fulfils what was foretold in the Old. *Dei Verbum* once again:

God, the inspirer and author of both Testaments, wisely arranged that the New Testament be hidden in the Old and the Old be made manifest in the New. For, though Christ established the new covenant in his blood (*Lk* 22:20; *1 Co* 11:25), still the books of the Old Testament with all their parts, caught up into the proclamation of the gospel, acquire and show forth their full meaning in the New Testament (*Mt* 5:17; *Lk* 24:27; *Rm* 16:25-26; *2 Co* 14:16) and in turn shed light on it and explain it. (*DV* 16)

3. How do we know which books make up the Old Testament and the New Testament?

The definitive list of the books of Sacred Scripture is known as the *canon* of Scripture. The canon is not mentioned anywhere in the Bible itself; instead it was received through Sacred Tradition by the early Church and, due to later disputes over some of the Old Testament books, came to be definitively settled by the Church's authority. The earliest authoritative canon was given by Pope Damasus at a local synod held in Rome in the year 382. Several subsequent synods in other locations later ratified the same canon, and the Catholic Church has never wavered from it. However, since the canon comes to us through Sacred Tradition, some non-Catholic Christian groups that don't recognise Sacred Tradition have disputed that canon.

The most notable of these disputes occurred at the dawn of Protestantism. During the Reformation in the sixteenth century, primarily for doctrinal reasons Protestants removed seven books (labelling them as *apocrypha*) from the Old Testament: 1 and 2 Maccabees, Sirach, Wisdom,

Baruch, Tobit, and Judith, and parts of two others: Daniel and Esther. They did so even though these books (which came to be known as the *deuterocanonical* books) had been regarded as canonical since the beginning of Church history. There were also some Reformers who wanted to remove books from the New Testament as well (e.g., Martin Luther, who wanted to remove James), but they were unable to accomplish this in a widespread way.

Today, many Protestants do not realise that their Bibles are lacking so much text that was originally included. However, anyone who studies the authentic history of the canon must admit that this is the case. As Protestant church historian J. N. D. Kelly writes, "It should be observed that the Old Testament thus admitted as authoritative in the Church was somewhat bulkier and more comprehensive [than the Protestant Bible]… It always included, though with varying degrees of recognition, the so-called…deuterocanonical books,"[2] which are rejected by Protestants.

In response to Protestantism's widespread rejection of so much of the Old Testament, the Catholic Church re-affirmed the ancient canon, infallibly defining it at the Council of Trent in 1546.

Thus, the *Catechism* affirms to this day:

> It was by the apostolic tradition that the Church discerned which writings are to be included in the list of

the sacred books. This complete list is called the canon of Scripture. It includes 46 books for the Old Testament (45 if we count Jeremiah and Lamentations as one) and 27 for the New. (*CCC* 120)

Of course, anyone who rejects the authority of Sacred Tradition (or the Catholic Church) can add to the canon or remove from it whatever books he wants. But such a homemade canon would really be quite meaningless, as it would lack true authority.

4. What exactly is Sacred Tradition?

The word *tradition* comes down to us from the Latin *tradere* for "transmit" or "deliver" - literally, to "hand on." It was a term used in Roman law to denote the legal transfer of property. The Greek word for this is *paradosis,* which has the connotation of something deliberately handed on over a long period of time.

This is precisely what Jesus commanded the apostles to do with all that he handed on to *them* (see *Mt* 28:19-20). He even promised them the guidance of the Holy Spirit in order to accomplish this. At the Last Supper, Jesus promised the apostles that the Father "will give you another Counsellor, to be with you for ever... the Holy Spirit, whom the Father will send in my name, he will teach you all things, and bring to your remembrance all that I have said to you... he will guide you into all the truth" (*Jn* 14:16, 26; 16:13).

This is a critical assurance, since the apostles did not yet have a complete Bible from which to teach. As the *Catechism* explains:

> The Tradition here in question comes from the apostles and hands on what they received from Jesus' teaching and example and what they learned from the Holy Spirit. The first generation of Christians did not yet have a written New Testament, and the New Testament itself demonstrates the process of living Tradition. (*CCC* 83)

Of course, Jesus intended his teaching to be carefully transmitted, continually handed down until his return (see *Mt* 28:19-20). But nowhere does he indicate that this would be accomplished solely through a book. The apostles and their successors (likewise guided by the Holy Spirit) could also accomplish this through their oral preaching, as well as through their own example and observance.

> And so the apostolic preaching, which is expressed in a special way in the inspired books, was to be preserved by an unending succession of preachers until the end of time…Now what was handed on by the apostles includes everything which contributes toward the holiness of life and increase in faith of the peoples of God; and so the Church, in her teaching, life and worship, perpetuates and hands on to all generations all that she herself is, all that she believes. (*DV* 8)

Sacred Tradition, then, includes not only the doctrines handed down over the centuries but also all that encompasses the authentic life of the Church. Fr Yves Congar calls Sacred Tradition "the communication of the entire heritage of the apostles, effected in a different way from that of their writings."[3] Sacred Tradition is a living, breathing phenomenon that perpetuates the life of the Church down through the ages. It grows and develops as the Church grows and develops under the guidance of the Holy Spirit. *Dei Verbum* teaches:

> This tradition which comes from the Apostles develops in the Church with the help of the Holy Spirit. For there is a growth in the understanding of the realities and the words which have been handed down. This happens through the contemplation and study made by believers, who treasure these things in their hearts (see *Lk* 2:19, 51) through a penetrating understanding of the spiritual realities which they experience, and through the preaching of those who have received through Episcopal succession the sure gift of truth. For as the centuries succeed one another, the Church constantly moves forward toward the fullness of divine truth until the words of God reach their complete fulfilment in her. (*DV* 8)

Sacred Tradition carries on the Great Commission of the apostles to this day, and will continue to do so throughout the life of the Church until the end of time for the sake of the salvation of souls.

> The Father's self-communication made through his Word in the Holy Spirit, remains present and active in the Church: God, who spoke in the past, continues to converse with the Spouse of his beloved Son [the Church]. And the Holy Spirit, through whom the living voice of the Gospel rings out in the Church - and through her in the world - leads believers to the full truth, and makes the Word of Christ dwell in them in all its richness. (*CCC* 79)

5. Is Sacred Tradition mentioned in the Bible?

Many non-Catholic Christians mistakenly think that the Bible says that it alone - Sacred Scripture - is the sole rule of faith for Christians. However, nowhere in the Bible is this expressed or even implied. The Bible *does* express, however, that Sacred Tradition is crucially important for fully grasping the Christian faith. Jesus' commandment to the apostles at the end of Matthew's Gospel logically assumes the necessity of Sacred Tradition:

> Go therefore and make disciples of all nations, baptising them in the name of the Father and of the Son and of the Holy Spirit, and teaching them to obey all that I have commanded you. And remember, I am with you always, to the end of the age. (*Mt* 28:19-20)

Notice that Jesus did not tell the apostles to *write down* everything he had taught them. He simply commanded them to *teach* it. Much of this teaching later made its way into written form and became part of Sacred Scripture, but every bit of it was first - and still is - part of Sacred Tradition.

Consider St Luke's introduction to his Gospel, in which he explains why he is writing it. He points out that others have already committed certain things to writing, and he thinks it is a good idea to write down what his reader has been taught:

> In as much as many have undertaken to compile a narrative of the things which have been accomplished among us, just as they were delivered to us by those who from the beginning were eyewitnesses and ministers of the word, it seemed good to me also, having followed all things closely for some time past, to write an orderly account for you, most excellent Theophilus, that you may know the truth concerning the things of which you have been informed. (*Lk* 1:1-4)

Luke, then, commits to writing what has *already been taught*. That teaching is Sacred Tradition just as surely as Luke's Gospel will later be recognised as Sacred Scripture.

In his writings, St Paul provides even more explicit evidence of Sacred Tradition. For example, he tells the Corinthians, "I commend you because you remember me in everything and maintain the traditions even as I have delivered them to you" (*1 Co* 11:2). He also commands the Thessalonians, "So then, brethren, stand firm and hold to the traditions which you were taught by us, either by word of mouth or by letter" (*2 Th* 2:15). In this verse, Paul speaks of Sacred Tradition as being taught both orally and in writing. Much of his written teaching would later be canonised as Sacred Scripture, so this verse clearly demonstrates how Sacred Tradition preceded Sacred Scripture.

Paul even goes so far as to caution the Thessalonians about people who do *not* hold to the Sacred Tradition he taught them: "Now we command you, brethren, in the name of our Lord Jesus Christ, that you keep away from any brother who is living in idleness and not in accord with the tradition that you received from us" (*2 Th* 3:6).

Near the end of his ministry, Paul instructs Timothy to carry on the Sacred Tradition passed down to him: "Follow the pattern of the sound words which you have heard from me, in the faith and love which are in Christ Jesus; guard the truth that has been entrusted to you by the Holy Spirit who dwells within us" (*2 Tm* 1:13-14). To make sure that all this apostolic tradition would be passed down after the deaths of the apostles, he tells Timothy, "You, then, my son, be strong in the grace that is in Christ Jesus, and what you have heard from me before many witnesses entrust to faithful men who will be able to teach others also" (*2 Tm* 2:1-2). In this passage he refers to the first four generations of apostolic succession - his own generation, Timothy's generation, the generation Timothy will teach, and the generation they in turn will teach. Clearly, Paul had in mind that Sacred Tradition would continue to be an ordinary means of communicating the gospel.

Thus, Sacred Tradition is evidenced explicitly in the Bible, whereas the Bible (which is a product of Sacred Tradition) nowhere puts forth that the written word is to be the sole rule of the Christian faith. On the contrary, it is Sacred Tradition that is commanded time and again to be the ordinary, ongoing method of teaching the Christian faith.

6. Is there any *historical* evidence for Sacred Tradition actually being handed on from the apostles to their successors down through the centuries?

Beyond the biblical accounts of Sacred Tradition being handed on, many bishops and other Christians who were contemporaries of the apostles, or who lived in the centuries after them, continued to write books and letters similar to those in the New Testament. Many of these have been preserved and come down to us through history. These writings of the "Church Fathers" provide insight into what the early Christians believed. They offer historical proof that Sacred Tradition was, indeed, handed on from the apostles to their successors, and so on, and so on, to present day.

> The apostles entrusted the "sacred deposit" of the Faith (the *depositum fidei*), contained in Sacred Scripture and Tradition, to the whole of the Church. By adhering to this heritage the entire holy people, united to its pastors, remains always faithful to the teaching of the apostles, to the brotherhood, to the breaking of bread and the prayers. So, in maintaining, practising and professing the faith that has been handed on, there should be a remarkable harmony between the bishops and the faithful. (*CCC* 84)

The Church Fathers, who were early links in the chain of succession, recognised the necessity of the traditions that had been handed down from the apostles, and guarded them scrupulously, as abundant testimony indicates.

For example, St Irenaeus wrote in opposition to heresies in AD 189:

> [T]he Church, having received this preaching and this faith, although she is disseminated throughout the whole world, yet guarded it, as if she occupied but one house. She likewise believes these things just as if she had but one soul and one and the same heart; and harmoniously she proclaims them and teaches them and hands them down, as if she possessed but one mouth. For, while the languages of the world are diverse, nevertheless, the authority of the tradition is one and the same.[4]

Later he added: "It is possible, then, for everyone in every church, who may wish to know the truth, to contemplate the tradition of the apostles which has been made known throughout the whole world."[5]

In 225, Origen wrote: "The teaching of the Church has indeed been handed down through an order of succession from the apostles and remains in the churches even to the present time. That alone is to be believed as the truth which is in no way at variance with ecclesiastical and apostolic tradition."[6]

Writing in the early fourth century, Church historian Eusebius attested:

> Papias [AD 120], who is now mentioned by us, affirms that he received the sayings of the apostles from those who accompanied them, and he, moreover, asserts that he heard in person Aristion and the presbyter John. Accordingly, he mentions them frequently by name, and in his writings gives their traditions [concerning Jesus]....[There are] other passages of his in which he relates some miraculous deeds, stating that he acquired the knowledge of them from tradition.[7]
>
> At that time [AD 150] there flourished in the Church Hegesippus, whom we know from what has gone before, and Dionysius, bishop of Corinth, and another bishop, Pinytus of Crete, and besides these, Philip, and Apollinarius, and Melito, and Musanus, and Modestus,

> and, finally, Irenaeus. From them has come down to us in writing, the sound and orthodox faith received from tradition."[8]

Around 400, St Augustine wrote: "[T]here are many things which are observed by the whole Church, and therefore are fairly held to have been enjoined by the apostles, which yet are not mentioned in their writings."[9] He went on to call apostolic tradition "the fountain" that Christians should go back to for truth in matters of the Christian faith.[10]

In these examples and many others, we find clear historical evidence that the Christians of the first centuries of the Church did, indeed, hold fast to Sacred Tradition.

> The words of the holy fathers witness to the presence of this living tradition, whose wealth is poured into the practice and life of the believing and praying Church ...and thus God, who spoke of old, uninterruptedly converses with the bride of his beloved Son; and the Holy Spirit, through whom the living voice of the Gospel resounds in the Church, and through her, in the world, leads unto all truth those who believe and makes the word of Christ dwell abundantly in them. (*DV* 8)

7. Where can we find a list of all the teachings given to the apostles by divine revelation and contained in Sacred Tradition?

There is no such list, because some of the teachings have been passed down in implicit rather than explicit form, and it is impossible to list all of the implications of a set of doctrines.

Consider a similar question: Can any Christian list all the teachings divinely revealed in Sacred Scripture? Of course not! Our understanding of what is in Scripture (and Tradition) deepens and grows richer all the time; we have to contemplate it and apply it to new circumstances. In other words, teaching develops.

The opening verse of the book of Hebrews tells us, "In many and various ways God spoke of old to our fathers by the prophets." This was done fragmentarily, under various figures and symbols. Man was not given religious truth as though from a Sunday school teacher, nicely laid out and fully indexed. Doctrines had to be thought out, lived out in the liturgical life of the Church, even pieced together by the Fathers and ecumenical councils. In this way, the Church has gained an ever-deepening understanding of the deposit of faith that had been "once for all delivered" to it by Christ and the apostles (see *Jude* 3).

Non-Catholic Christians ordinarily admit that much. They recognise there has been a real development in doctrine. There was an initial message, much clouded at the Fall (*Gn* 3), and then a progressively fuller explanation of God's teachings as Israel was prepared for the Messiah, until the apostles were instructed by the Messiah himself. Jesus told the apostles that in the Old Testament "many prophets and righteous men longed to see what you see, and did not see it, and to hear what you hear, and did not hear it" (*Mt* 13:17).

Christians have always understood that at the close of the apostolic age - with the death of the last surviving apostle, John, around AD 100 - all of public revelation ceased (*CCC* 66-67, 73). Christ fulfilled the Old Testament law (*Mt* 5:17) and is the ultimate teacher of humanity: "You have one teacher, the Messiah" (*Mt* 23:10). The apostles recognised that their task was to pass on, intact, the faith given to them by Christ: "[A]nd what you have heard from me before many witnesses entrust to faithful men who will be able to teach others also" (2 *Tm* 2:2); "But as for you, continue in what you have learned and have firmly believed, knowing from whom you learned it" (*2 Tm* 3:14).

However, this closure to public revelation doesn't mean there can't be progress in the understanding of what has been entrusted to the Church - and ever fuller flowering of the deposit of revelation. Anyone interested in Christianity will ask of a given revealed truth, "What does this teaching imply? How does it relate to other teachings?"

A good example of why this is so can be found in the *Monothelite* controversy. The Monothelites were seventh-century heretics who claimed that Jesus had (and has) only one will, the divine. The orthodox position, defined at the Third Council of Constantinople (680-681), is that Jesus also has a human will that is distinct from - but never in conflict with - his divine will. The Bible doesn't teach this in so many words. Neither did the writings of the earliest Church Fathers explicitly state that Christ has a human will distinct from but in harmony with his divine will. That doctrine was not handed on from the apostles in explicit form, but it was handed on in *implicit* form.

The apostles taught, as the Bible and the Church Fathers indicate, that Jesus was fully human and fully divine. This contains the implicit teaching of two wills, because if Christ is fully human, he must have a human will, and if he is fully divine, he must have a divine will. For Christ to lack one or the other would make him either not be fully human or not be fully divine. Because of Christ's supreme holiness and the unity of his person, his human and divine wills could never be in conflict.

Most non-Catholic Christians fully agree. They acknowledge that the doctrine of the two wills of Christ must be accepted as something coming to us from the apostles, even though it did not come in explicit form. It was a legitimate doctrinal development that emerged when a heresy struck and the Church sought a deeper, more explicit understanding of what it had already implicitly received.

Thus the Church does not try to make an exhaustive list of implicit doctrines, but allows new implications within the apostolic deposit to be realised over the course of time, as the Holy Spirit leads the Church into all truth (see *Jn* 16:13). If the Church did try to make such a list, it would be attempting to run ahead of the Holy Spirit by forcing the process of doctrinal development to a sudden and premature end. If the Church, for instance, had tried to make such a list before the outbreak of the Monothelite controversy, the list would not have included the proposition, "Christ has a human will distinct from but entirely in harmony with his divine will."

No one would have thought to include that proposition because no dispute had arisen about the issue. Once the Monothelites appeared and the Church was pushed into realising what Christ's full humanity implies, the Monothelites could have claimed, "You can't say that Christ has two wills. The list of apostolic teachings doesn't mention such a doctrine." If it had presumed to have already compiled an exhaustive list of the teachings of Sacred Tradition, the Church would have had no way to put down the Monothelite heresy and many others.

8. Can Sacred Tradition contradict the Bible?

Because it is the word of God, Sacred Tradition is inerrant, and because it is inerrant, it can never contradict Sacred Scripture, which is also inerrant. *Human* tradition may contain mistakes, but Sacred Tradition does not. Likewise, though our understanding of it can grow and develop over time, Sacred Tradition cannot be changed any more than the Bible can be changed. They both come from God, whose truth is unchanging.

Clearly, it is crucial to be able to distinguish between Sacred Tradition, which is revealed by God and unchangeable, and human traditions, which can come and go over time. The *Catechism* notes:

> [Sacred] Tradition is to be distinguished from the various theological, disciplinary, liturgical or devotional traditions, born in the local churches over time. These are the particular forms, adapted to different places and times, in which the great Tradition is expressed. In the light of Tradition, these traditions can be retained, modified or even abandoned under the guidance of the Church's Magisterium. (83)

The key to determining which traditions are sacred and which are merely human is the same as the key to telling which writings are sacred and which are merely human. The authoritative Magisterium - the official teaching authority - of the Church recognises the "canon," so to speak, of Sacred Tradition, just as it recognised the canon of Sacred Scripture. As we know, Catholics recognise that those doctrinal and moral teachings taught by the Church since the beginning of Christian history were given by Jesus to the apostles and handed on by them to their successors down through the centuries. The Church recognises these teachings, and those that have developed from them, as Sacred Tradition.

Other Catholic traditions, more aptly called *ecclesiastical* traditions (or disciplines or customs), are "man-made" in the sense that Christians developed them over the centuries as means to better live out their Christian faith. All Christian communities - not just Catholics - have human traditions in one form or another. But Sacred Tradition, as a direct expression of the authority Jesus gave to the apostles and their successors, is different. Whatever the Catholic Church teaches, it is bound to fidelity to Sacred Tradition and Sacred Scripture. It cannot sanction just anything it chooses, but only that which is in accord with what it has been given. Sacred Tradition comes from God so, as such, it may not be altered by men. Other traditions originated with the Church's pastoral and disciplinary authority and, therefore, may change.

Admittedly, this can sometimes be confusing - even for Catholics. For example, consider the Church's teaching concerning the male-only priesthood. Some Catholics (mistakenly) believe that the Church can change this doctrine and that women can and should be ordained as priests. In other words, they believe this doctrine to be a changeable discipline.

Of course informed Catholics recognise that the male-only priesthood is not only *implicit* in Sacred Scripture (in the Bible, Christ chooses only men as priests, and the apostles did likewise) but it is also *explicit* in Sacred Tradition. In fact, quite recently in Church history Pope John Paul II confirmed this doctrine in his 1994 apostolic letter *Ordinatio Sacerdotalis*, and the Church's Congregation for the Doctrine of the Faith subsequently attested to its certitude, and its place in Sacred Tradition: "This teaching requires definitive assent, since, founded on the written Word of God, and from the beginning constantly preserved and applied in the Tradition of the Church, it has been set forth infallibly by the ordinary and universal Magisterium."[11]

In contrast to the doctrine of the male-only priesthood is the discipline of celibacy in the priesthood. It is widely known that, in general, throughout most of the Catholic Church only men who are willing to commit to lifelong celibacy can be ordained to the priesthood. However, mandatory priestly celibacy is not a revealed doctrine of the Church. It does not come down to us by the authority of Sacred Scripture or Sacred Tradition. It is more accurately described as an ecclesiastical tradition, and, as such, it could theoretically change - the Church could choose to ordain married men. In fact, it already does so, in certain cases.[12]

9. Doesn't Vatican II say that Sacred Scripture - and, therefore, Sacred Tradition by association - is inerrant in only a very limited way?

No document from the Second Vatican Council limits Sacred Scripture's inerrancy. Confusion sometimes arises, though, in regard to this statement in *Dei Verbum*:

> Therefore, since everything asserted by the inspired authors or sacred writers must be held to be asserted by the Holy Spirit, it follows that the books of Scripture must be acknowledged as teaching solidly, faithfully, and without error that truth which God wanted put into the sacred writings for the sake of our salvation. (11)

Proponents of so-called "limited inerrancy" claim that the last clause of this paragraph is restrictive: that inerrancy extends *only* to those parts of Scripture pertaining to our salvation. However, in order to better grasp an authentic interpretation of this clause, it is helpful to understand that it - and all of the documents of Vatican II for that matter - must be interpreted in proper context, in light of the historical, authoritative teaching of the Magisterium. Pope Benedict XVI said as much in 2005:

> On the one hand, there is an interpretation that I would call "a hermeneutic of discontinuity and rupture"... On the other, there is the "hermeneutic of reform", of

> renewal in the continuity of the one subject-Church which the Lord has given to us. She is a subject which increases in time and develops, yet always remaining the same, the one subject of the journeying People of God... The Church, both before and after the Council, was and is the same Church, one, holy, catholic and apostolic, journeying on through time.[13]

In other words, *Dei Verbum* along with *all* documents of the Magisterium of the Catholic Church must be interpreted in continuity with what the same Magisterium has continually taught in the past.

In 1893, Pope Leo XIII issued the most comprehensive magisterial treatment of Scripture interpretation the world had yet seen. *Providentissimus Deus* was a landmark encyclical that sought to correct the many errors about Scripture then circulating the world. In it, Pope Leo pointedly affirms the *unrestricted* inerrancy of Sacred Scripture:

> For all the books which the Church receives as sacred and canonical, are written wholly and entirely, with all their parts, at the dictation of the Holy Ghost; and so far is it from being possible that any error can co-exist with inspiration, that inspiration not only is essentially incompatible with error, but excludes and rejects it as absolutely and necessarily as it is impossible that God Himself, the supreme Truth, can utter that which is not true... It follows that those who maintain that an error is

possible in any genuine passage of the sacred writings, either pervert the Catholic notion of inspiration, or make God the author of such error. (20-21)

In 1920, Pope Benedict XV re-affirmed Pope Leo XIII's teaching in his own encyclical, *Spiritus Paraclitus,* and Pius XII did likewise in 1943 with *Divino Afflante Spiritu.*

Dei Verbum, then, must be interpreted within the context of, and with fidelity to, these prior documents. In fact, the language of *Dei Verbum* eleven is taken directly from them, and its footnotes even refer to them. Vatican II clearly did not intend to contradict them! The theological commission at Vatican II even made a point of stating that the Latin term *salutaris* ("for the sake of our salvation") does *not* mean that only the "salvific" truths of the Bible are inspired or that the Bible as a whole is not the Word of God.

If the whole of Scripture is inspired - if what the biblical writer asserts the Holy Spirit asserts - and if the Holy Spirit can't err, then biblical inerrancy cannot be limited just to certain parts of the Bible.

In *Divino Afflante Spiritu*, Pope Pius XII uses the *incarnational analogy* to explain this: "For as the substantial Word of God became like to men in all things, except sin, so the words of God, expressed in human language, are made like to human speech in every respect, except error" (37). This analogy essentially compares the Word of God in Scripture to the Word of God made flesh, Jesus. Just as the Word took on human flesh in Jesus, the Word took on human language in Sacred Scripture. And just as Jesus is fully human yet fully divine, Scripture is authored both by human authors and the divine author. Finally, just as Jesus is like men in all ways except sin, Scripture is like human language in all ways except error. This analogy may be equally applied to Sacred Tradition as well.

10. I agree that Church Tradition has authority, but isn't the Bible the only *infallible* authority?

It is important to distinguish between the terms *infallible* and *inerrant*. Non-Catholics often claim that the Bible is infallible but that is a misuse of the term. *Infallible* means unable to make a mistake or to teach error, and the term is used in reference to people, not inanimate objects like books.

Normally, human beings are fallible - capable of making mistakes - but in order to preserve his teachings over time Jesus gave the charism (gift) of infallibility to certain people in the Church in certain circumstances. Such infallibility means that the pope and bishops are protected from error when they proclaim by a definitive act a doctrine pertaining to faith or morals (see *CCC* 891). This does not mean, however, that they are otherwise inerrant, are inspired by the Holy Spirit to deliver new revelation, or are personally *impeccable* (incapable of sin).

And so it is not accurate to say that the Bible is infallible. Rather, as discussed above (see question 9), the Bible is *inerrant*. Everything the Bible asserts, correctly understood, is true and therefore without error.

Indeed, Sacred Scripture and Sacred Tradition, having God as their source, are both inerrant. Therefore, when the correct understanding of a doctrinal matter is at question, both Scripture and Tradition may be consulted in order to settle the matter. After all, both are the word of God and they never contradict each other.

For example, the doctrine of baptismal regeneration is found several places in Scripture, such as in John 3:5, where Jesus says, "Unless one is born of water and the Spirit, he cannot enter the kingdom of God." But because Jesus uses the metaphor for baptism, "born of water and the Spirit," many Protestants over history have tried to deny that it is a reference to baptism at all, and have claimed that baptismal regeneration is false. This is disproven through the Sacred Tradition preserved in the writings of the Church Fathers, who not only teach baptismal regeneration but also unanimously interpret John 3:5 as referring to baptism.[14]

Not all Protestants disagree with Sacred Tradition on every matter. In cases where they agree, however, it is not because they recognise the authority of Sacred Tradition, but because their personal interpretations of Sacred Scripture (their own personal *traditions*, you might say) just happen to agree with it - or have been shaped by it without their realising. The disunity among the world's Protestant churches is due, at least in part, to Protestants following their principle of *sola scriptura*. Even when sin and pride are excluded from the equation, Protestants still interpret the Bible differently on important issues - sometimes even on questions (such as the nature of baptism) directly related to salvation. This points to a *defective method of discerning what it is that God has revealed*, not merely to defective discerners.

As doctrine develops, there sometimes arises the need to settle opposing views authoritatively. This is where infallibility is particularly valuable. Over the long history of the Church, heresies have been weeded out and doctrine has authoritatively developed under the assurance of the charism of infallibility.

When trying to judge disputed doctrines, non-Catholic Christians do not enjoy such assurances as the inerrancy of Sacred Tradition and the charism of infallibility provide. Instead, they must rely on their own fallible interpretations of Scripture. For example, consider the discipline of priestly celibacy. As we saw earlier, this practice is a matter of Church discipline, not doctrine. But some Protestants read the Bible and decide for themselves that the discipline is forbidden by Scripture.

To prove this, they will often cite two verses: "Now a bishop must be above reproach, the husband or wife, temperate, sensible, dignified, hospitable, an apt teacher"

(*1 Tm* 3:2) and "Let deacons be the husband of one wife, and let them manage their children and their households well" (*1 Tm* 3:12). They interpret these verses so literally as to mean that bishops and deacons - and priests for that matter - *must* be married.

If the Bible alone were the only authority we had to settle the question of whether the priesthood could be restricted to unmarried men, such an interpretation of these verses might be the right one, or it might not. "Husband of one wife" could be taken as forbidding ordination to unmarried men. Or it could be about forbidding ordination to men with more than one wife, or to widows or divorcés who have remarried, and have nothing to do with whether celibacy is an "unbiblical" discipline. And in either case, it could be a general exhortation that's not exclusively binding. Especially if we take those verses together with other verses that seem to *recommend* the celibate state,[15] Scripture alone doesn't seem to answer the question one way or the other.

Fortunately, it doesn't have to. Catholics do not rely on Scripture alone for settling such matters. Sacred Tradition - expressed in the beliefs and practices that the early Church received from the apostles - fills out and interprets the revelation of Sacred Scripture on the question, and authoritatively settles the matter for us. Priestly celibacy is a noble, permissible, but not doctrinally required discipline, and this is true matter how any one individual interprets the Bible today or a thousand years from today.

11. The Catholic Church claims to be the guardian of the Bible, but didn't it demonstrate hostility towards Scripture when it added unscriptural books to the Old Testament, namely the Apocrypha?

As we briefly noted in a prior answer, the seven books in question - Tobit, Judith, 1 and 2 Maccabees, Wisdom, Sirach, and Baruch - are properly called the *deuterocanonical* books, not "apocrypha." (Also included among these are parts of Esther and Daniel.) The term apocrypha refers to books of dubious authenticity, but this description does not apply to the deuterocanonical books.

What does deuterocanonical mean? The term technically means "second canon," but this is somewhat of a misnomer. The *Catholic Encyclopedia* explains:

> The terms *protocanonical* and *deuterocanonical*, of frequent usage among Catholic theologians and exegetes, require a word of caution…[I]t would be wrong to infer from them that the Church successively possessed two distinct biblical canons. Only in a partial and restricted way may we speak of a first and second canon. Protocanonical (*protos*, "first") is a conventional word denoting those sacred writings which have been always received by Christendom without dispute. The protocanonical books of the Old Testament correspond with those of the Bible of the Hebrews

> and the Old Testament as received by Protestants. The deuterocanonical (*deuteros*, "second") are those whose scriptural character was contested in some quarters, but which long ago gained a secure footing in the Bible of the Catholic Church, though those of the Old Testament are classed by Protestants as the "Apocrypha."[16]

Use of the terms protocanonical and deuterocanonical only came about in the sixteenth century, when the Protestant Reformers contested the canon of Scripture. The Church had never understood these terms to denote superior and inferior kinds of biblical books. The truth is, portions of these books contradict elements of Protestant doctrine (for example, 2 Maccabees 12 which clearly supports prayers for the dead and a belief in purgatory), and the Reformers therefore needed some excuse to eliminate them from the canon. But the earliest Christians, the apostles, even Jesus himself attested to their canonicity by quoting from the Septuagint, a Greek translation of the Hebrew scriptures that contained these seven books. More importantly, the New Testament alludes to them. A prime example of this is Hebrews 11:35, which is an indisputable reference to 2 Maccabees 7.

As we saw earlier, the canon of the entire Bible was essentially settled around the turn of the fourth century. Up until that time, there had been disagreement over the canon, and there existed around ten different proposed lists that didn't correspond exactly to what the Bible now contains. To settle the matter, the Church formally identified the canon in no fewer than five instances: the Synod of Rome (382), the Council of Hippo (393), the Council of Carthage (397), a letter from Pope Innocent I to Exsuperius, bishop of Toulouse (405), and the Second Council of Carthage (419). In every instance, the identified canon was identical to what Catholic Bibles contain today. In other words, from the end of the fourth century on, *in practice* Christians accepted the Catholic Church's decision in this matter.

By the time of the Reformation, Christians had been using the same seventy-three books in their Bibles (forty-six in the Old Testament, twenty-seven in the New Testament) for more than 1100 years. This practice changed with Martin Luther, who in the sixteenth century dropped the deuterocanonical books on nothing more than his own say-so, with Protestantism as a whole eventually following his lead. This led the Council of Trent (1545-1563) to affirm the full canon of Scripture for a second time, giving rise to the use of the term *deuterocanonical*.

Sola scriptura, one of the two "pillars" of the Protestant Reformation, states in part that nothing can be added to *or taken away from* God's word. History shows that Protestants violated their own doctrine. It was they who showed hostility to the integrity of Sacred Scripture - by subtracting from it.

12. Isn't the Muratorian Fragment proof that the canon of Scripture was settled long before the fourth century, contrary to what the Catholic Church claims?

The Muratorian Fragment (so called because it represents only a portion of the actual second-century document discovered in 1740 by Lodovico Antonio Muratori) is the oldest extant listing of New Testament-era books revered by early Christians. It was written sometime between 155 and 200. Patristic scholars believe the unknown author originally wrote the list in Greek (since the Latin is very poor), but the oldest copy available is an eighth-century Latin manuscript.

Protestants who try to argue for an earlier dating of the canon in order to diminish the importance of the Catholic Church in establishing it will sometimes cite this list in their arguments. But although the Muratorian Fragment is important for studying how the early Church developed the New Testament canon, it does not give exactly the same list of books that was later adopted as canonical at the synod of Rome and councils of Hippo and Carthage. The Muratorian Fragment is just that: a portion of a larger list of books which were considered canonical or quasi-canonical by some Christians during the second century.

The Fragment itself provides us with a good, though incomplete, idea of this early list of books. Virtually the entire New Testament canon as we know it is represented:

the Gospels of Luke and John (preceded by what seems to be an allusion to the Gospel of Mark), Acts, 1 and 2 Corinthians, Galatians, Romans, Ephesians, Philippians, Colossians, 1 and 2 Thessalonians, Philemon, Titus, 1 and 2 Timothy, Jude, two letters of John (since the fragment simply says "the two ascribed to John," we don't know which two of his three letters are meant), and Revelation.

The unknown author includes non-canonical books in this line-up as well: the so-called Pauline Epistles to the Laodiceans and to the Alexandrians (about which the Fragment's author expresses his conviction that they were not authored by Paul), the Wisdom Written by the Friends of Solomon in His Honour, the Apocalypse of Peter, and the Shepherd (written by Hermas). The Fragment's list is cut short with a final, enigmatic phrase that may indicate that the author had gone on to include still other non-inspired writings: "Those also who wrote the new book of psalms for Marcion, together with Basilides, the founder of the Asian Cataphrygians."

And so, although the Muratorian Fragment lists most of the New Testament books, it is missing a few (for example, Matthew and James), and it adds several works that are not inspired.

Although the Fragment came close, it did not represent the actual canon of inspired Scripture that would later be settled in accordance with Sacred Tradition by the authority of the Church. Indeed, there is no internal evidence in the document that it even sought to represent any kind of official canon that was regarded by the Church as binding.

In the first four centuries of the Church, many books, such as the seven letters of Ignatius, the Letter of Clement (the fourth pope) to the Corinthians, the Didache, and the Shepherd, were revered by many Christians as inspired but were later excluded from the canon of Scripture. It was not until the Synod of Rome and the subsequent Councils of Hippo and Carthage that the Catholic Church defined which books made it into the New Testament and which didn't. Probably the council fathers studied the (complete) Muratorian Fragment as well as other documents, including, of course, the books in question themselves, but it was not until these much later councils that the Church officially settled the issue.

The plain fact of the matter is that the canon of the Bible was not fully settled in the first couple centuries of the Church. It was settled only after repeated (and perhaps heated) discussions, and the final listing was determined in the fourth century, by Catholic bishops in communion with the pope. This is an inescapable fact, no matter how many people wish to escape from it.

13. If Church documents are sometimes infallible, don't they in effect add to the Bible, in violation of John's warning in Revelation?

The Catholic Church has such a high view of Sacred Scripture that we believe in the Church's authority to produce infallible magisterial documents without making them the equivalent of additional Scripture. Simply being infallible and binding does not make a document equal to Scripture, because Scripture is qualitatively something more: it is the inspired, inerrant word of God. It is divine revelation given over a certain period of time and then definitively ended.

Even the most solemn and authoritative magisterial documents are purely human writings, not divine; they are *about* divine revelation, but are not themselves revealed. God is not their author, but rather a kind of editor; he does not inscribe truth into them, but only keeps error out. The notion that any inerrant document amounts to additional Scripture would betray a shockingly *low* view of Scripture, one which defines Scripture merely as that which is authoritative and without error.

Beyond this, the very charge of adding to the Bible presupposes that the writing of Scripture has ended - a doctrine that is contained in Sacred Tradition and affirmed by the authoritative teaching of the Church, but *nowhere* made explicit in Sacred Scripture itself. Ironically, this charge against the Church assumes a doctrine that is explicitly taught *only* in Church documents expounding Sacred Tradition!

The Catholic Church continues to teach this doctrine to the present day. "The Christian economy, therefore, since it is the new and definitive Covenant, will never pass away; and no new public revelation is to be expected before the glorious manifestation of our Lord Jesus Christ." (*CCC* 66-67)

Even so, Sacred Tradition continues to develop, and the Church grows to understand it more fully. This sometimes is evidenced by magisterial documents. The *Catechism* continues: "Yet even if revelation is already complete, it has not been made completely explicit; it remains for Christian faith gradually to grasp its full significance over the course of the centuries."

But it is important to understand that the Church does not equate this development to adding to the Bible. Not even private revelations made by God to Christians throughout history add to the word of God:

> Throughout the ages, there have been so-called "private" revelations, some of which have been recognised by the authority of the Church. They do not belong, however, to the deposit of faith. It is not their role to improve or complete Christ's definitive Revelation, but to help live more fully by it in a certain period of history. Guided

> by the Magisterium of the Church, the *sensus fidelium* knows how to discern and welcome in these revelations whatever constitutes an authentic call of Christ or his saints to the Church. (*CCC* 67)

Indeed, in that same passage the *Catechism* recognises the dangers of claiming to be able to add new revelation to the deposit of faith, as some quasi-Christian groups do:

> Christian faith cannot accept "revelations" that claim to surpass or correct the Revelation of which Christ is the fulfilment, as is the case in certain non-Christian religions and also in certain recent sects which base themselves on such "revelations."

Of final note, it should be mentioned that the warning in Revelation 22:18-19 does not actually refer to writing additional Scripture, but to tampering with "the words of this scroll," i.e., the Book of Revelation itself:

> I warn everyone who hears the words of the prophecy of this book: if any one adds to them, God will add to him the plagues described in this book, and if any one takes away from the words of the book of this prophecy, God will take away his share in the tree of life and in the holy city, which are described in this book.

Similar warnings can be found in the Old Testament, long before the end of the age of revelation. For example, Deuteronomy 4:2 states: "You shall not add to the word which I command you, nor take from it; that you may keep the commandments of the LORD your God which I command you."

If this verse had been interpreted the same way many non-Catholics interpret Revelation 22:18-19 today, then nothing written after the book of Deuteronomy could be considered as Sacred Scripture!

14. Isn't the Bible all we really need to evangelise the world?

According to Sacred Scripture itself, the preferred method of communicating the word of God is not in writing but by word of mouth. Much of the Old Testament was known and transmitted orally for centuries before it was written down. St John emphasised the preference for spreading the gospel by Sacred Tradition when he wrote, "Though I have much to write to you, I would rather not use paper and ink, but I hope to come to see you and talk with you face to face, so that our joy may be complete" (*2 Jn* 12).

It might be helpful to imagine yourself living at the dawn of Christianity. There were nearly three decades between the Crucifixion and the writing of the first epistles of the New Testament, and nearly five more decades before the last New Testament book was written. Many Christians believed in Jesus and even died for his sake, without ever encountering the words of St Paul - for the simple reason that Paul had not yet written them! Indeed, before Paul was even converted he witnessed and approved of the death of one of those martyrs: St Stephen. Was Stephen's faith, or the faith of any of these early Christians, deficient somehow because most of the New Testament didn't exist yet? On the contrary - Stephen and others were so well grounded in the Faith handed on through Sacred Tradition that they were willing to suffer death for it.

All this is not to deny the value of the written word. Rather, it is to demonstrate the power of Sacred Tradition, which came long before a word of the New Testament was ever written. Jesus himself wrote none of the New Testament. He taught orally. He established a living Church founded on Peter and the apostles, and he told them to *preach*. We see in Paul's epistles how anxious he is about the welfare of the local churches he has established and how he wishes he could be there with them *in person* to guide and teach. Consider these verses:

> For I long to see you, that I may impart to you some spiritual gift to strengthen you. (*Rm* 1:11)

> I hope to see you in passing as I go to Spain, and to be sped on my journey there by you, once I have enjoyed your company for a little. (*Rm* 15:24)

> For I do not want to see you now just in passing; I hope to spend some time with you, if the Lord permits. (*1 Co* 16: 7)

> But since we were bereft of you, brethren, for a short time, in person not in heart, we endeavoured the more eagerly and with great desire to see you face to face. (*1 Th* 2:17)

> We long to see you…praying earnestly night and day that we may see you face to face and supply what is lacking in your faith (*1 Th* 3:6, 10). Clearly, Paul understood the value of human interaction when teaching the Christian faith! Sacred Tradition provides this in a way the Sacred Scripture alone docs not.

Not only did much of the New Testament not exist for the first generation of Christians - for over two and a half centuries there was no authoritatively settled canon of Scripture. As we saw, there was some common consensus that certain books were inspired, but there was also dispute and error. Christians during that time did not have a complete and authoritative Bible, but they *did* have a living and authoritative Tradition from the apostles. The faithful, like us today, had to rely on the authority Jesus gave to the leaders of the Church and their successors. It was that authority that eventually compiled the Bible, discerning which books to include and which not.

The Bible is a testament to the oral tradition that was alive and already at work from the beginning of the Church. Sacred Scripture is itself a product of the Sacred Tradition of the Church. And it is through the continual handing-on of Tradition that Scripture is authoritatively interpreted. "Through the same tradition the Church's full canon of the sacred books is known, and the sacred writings themselves are more profoundly understood and unceasingly made active in her." (*DV* 8)

15. Once the New Testament books were written down, didn't this do away with the need for Sacred Tradition?

Much, though not all, of Sacred Tradition made its way into inspired writing under the influence of the Holy Spirit, but it did not thereby cease to be Sacred Tradition, or cease to be valuable as such.

One reason for this is that even after much of Tradition became captured in Scripture, *interpretation* of that Scripture would continue to be an issue. In fact, it was an issue from the earliest days of Christianity. The New Testament itself provides evidence of this. For example, St Peter wrote, "There are some things in [Paul's letters] hard to understand, which the ignorant and unstable twist to their own destruction, as they do the other scriptures" (*2 P* 3:16). Here we see that even during the apostolic era there was concern about misguided interpretations of the scriptures. Peter goes on to warn Christians, "You therefore, beloved, knowing this beforehand, beware lest you be carried away with the error of lawless men and lose your own stability" (3:17).

The early Christians were hearing many interpretations of Scripture, and they couldn't *all* be correct. Sacred Tradition provided the way to discern the correct understanding. Early Christians knew they could trust Peter's teaching because he was one of Jesus's apostles, those who Jesus first appointed with authority to teach. They recognised that the apostles were sent by Christ endowed with special authority to teach in his name.[17]

Peter also taught, "First of all you must understand this, that no prophecy of Scripture is a matter of one's own interpretation, because no prophecy ever came by the impulse of man, but men moved by the Holy Spirit spoke from God" (*2 P* 1:20-21). In other words, just as Scripture was written under the inspiration of the Holy Spirit, the only guarantee of its authentic interpretation is by those who have the Holy Spirit's guidance: the apostles and their successors. It is their apostolic teaching that is called Sacred Tradition.

Peter went on to warn about those who taught without authority: "[T]here will be false teachers among you, who will secretly bring in destructive heresies, even denying the Master who bought them, bringing upon themselves swift destruction" (*2 P* 2:1). Even in the first century the problem of false teaching and heresy was an issue.

Accordingly, the author of the Letter to the Hebrews writes:

> Remember your leaders, those who spoke to you the word of God; consider the outcome of their life, and imitate their faith. Jesus Christ is the same yesterday and today and forever. Do not be led away by diverse and strange teachings; for it is well that the heart be strengthened by grace, not by foods, which have not benefited their adherents...Obey your leaders and submit to them; for they are keeping watch over your souls, as men who will have to give account. Let them do this joyfully, and not sadly, for that would be of no advantage to you. (*Heb* 13:7-9, 17)

Notice that there is no mention of a Bible here. Instead the author exhorts his readers to hold to the spoken word - Sacred Tradition - passed on by those with authority. The *Catechism* elaborates:

> No one can give himself the mandate and the mission to proclaim the gospel. The one sent by the Lord does not speak and act on his own authority, but by virtue of Christ's authority; not as a member of the community, but speaking to it in the name of Christ (*CCC* 875)

The early Fathers of the Church, who lived after the New Testament books were written but before the canon was settled, also attest to the necessity of Sacred Tradition in getting the Faith right. For example, Cyprian of Carthage writes in 253 about a false teacher of his day: "Novatian is not in the Church; nor can he be reckoned as a bishop, who, succeeding to no one, and despising the evangelical and apostolic tradition, sprang from himself."[18]

Basil the Great writes in 375:

> Of the dogmas and messages preserved in the Church, some we possess from written teaching and others we receive from the tradition of the apostles, handed on to us in mystery. In respect to piety, both are of the same force. No one will contradict any of these, no one, at any rate, who is even moderately versed in matters ecclesiastical. Indeed, were we to try to reject unwritten customs as having no great authority, we would unwittingly injure the gospel in its vitals; or rather, we would reduce the message to a mere term.[19]

Similarly, that same year Epiphanius of Salamis writes: "It is needful also to make use of tradition, for not everything can be gotten from Sacred Scripture. The holy apostles handed down some things in the scriptures, other things in tradition."[20]

Thus, Sacred Scripture does not stand alone. It was never intended to. The assurance of correctly passing on the Faith comes through Sacred Tradition handed on by those with teaching authority.

> The task of giving an authentic interpretation of the word of God, whether in its written form or in the form

of tradition, has been entrusted to the living teaching office of the Church alone. Its authority in this matter is exercised in the name of Jesus Christ This means that the task of interpretation has been entrusted to the bishops in communion with the successor of Peter, the bishop of Rome. (*CCC* 85)

16. Maybe we needed Tradition before the biblical canon was finally decided, but after it was - after we know for sure what was Scripture and what wasn't - shouldn't *that* have made Tradition unnecessary?

Sincere, intelligent, faithful Christians of all kinds study their Bibles, listen to Bible teaching, and pray for the grace of correct interpretation, yet come to different conclusions about what Scripture has to say about many important topics. They all genuinely believe their interpretations are *the* correct ones, and can't be convinced of any flaw in their understanding. Get just about any two of these people together in conversation about Scripture, and chances are they will not see eye to eye on everything.

So, even with a settled canon (and remember, even the canon is not exactly the same for Catholics and Protestants), the need for Sacred Tradition remains. Biblical doctrine is neither perfectly clear nor self-interpreting. Tradition helps draw out and correctly identify Scripture's true meaning.

Furthermore, even the complete canon of Sacred Scripture can never fully suffice for passing on the Faith. St John wrote:

> Now Jesus did many other signs in the presence of the disciples, which are not written in this book; but these are written that you may believe that Jesus is the Christ, the Son of God, and that believing you may have life in his name ...there are also many other things which Jesus did; were every one of them to be written, I suppose that the world itself could not contain the books that would be written. (*Jn* 20:30-31; 21:25)

Even taken in their most gentle sense, those words inescapably mean that in no way can the Bible be taken as the complete record of everything Jesus did, said, or taught. The early Christian leaders and writers clearly understood this and its implications. Writing in the early fifth century, not long after the canon of Scripture was settled, St John Chrysostom (c. 347-407) comments on a verse we have already looked at, 2 Thessalonians 2:15:

> From this it is clear that [the apostles] did not hand down everything by letter, but there is much also that was not written. Like that which was written, the unwritten too is worthy of belief. So let us regard the tradition of the Church also as worthy of belief. Is it a tradition? Seek no further.[21]

So, even after the canon of Sacred Scripture was settled, Sacred Tradition was still deemed necessary for discerning the fullness of the Christian faith. St Vincent of Lerins wrote in 434:

> With great zeal and closest attention, therefore, I frequently inquired of many men, eminent for their holiness and doctrine, how I might, in a concise and, so to speak, general and ordinary way, distinguish the truth of the Catholic faith from the falsehood of heretical depravity.
>
> I received almost always the same answer from all of them - that if I or anyone else wanted to expose the frauds and escape the snares of the heretics who rise up, and to remain intact and in sound faith, it would be necessary, with the help of the Lord, to fortify that faith in a twofold manner: first, of course, by the authority of divine law [Sacred Scripture] and then by the tradition of the Catholic Church.
>
> Here, perhaps, someone may ask: "If the canon of the scriptures be perfect and in itself more than suffices for everything, why is it necessary that the authority of ecclesiastical interpretation be joined to it?' Because, quite plainly, Sacred Scripture, by reason of its own depth, is not accepted by everyone as having one and the same meaning....

> Thus, because of so many distortions of such various errors, it is highly necessary that the line of prophetic and apostolic interpretation be directed in accord with the norm of the ecclesiastical and Catholic meaning.[22]

Of course, all of this remains true, especially in our time when so many Christians reject Sacred Tradition and have nothing against which to measure their interpretation of Scripture. Most of Sacred Tradition contains the same material that is found in Sacred Scripture, only in different form. This makes the two useful for interpreting and confirming each other.

> This living transmission, accomplished in the Holy Spirit, is called tradition, since it is distinct from Sacred Scripture, though closely connected to it. Through tradition, the Church, in her doctrine, life and worship, perpetuates and transmits to every generation all that she herself is, all that she believes. (*CCC* 78)

17. Didn't Jesus say that any tradition that contradicts Scripture is false, meaning that tradition is inferior to Scripture?

Sola scriptura adherents are quick to point out that the Bible condemns "tradition." For example, St Mark tells us of an incident when Jesus denounced certain tradition

> Now when the Pharisees gathered together to [Jesus],

> with some of the scribes, who had come from Jerusalem, they saw that some of his disciples ate with hands defiled, that is, unwashed. (For the Pharisees, and all the Jews, do not eat unless they wash their hands, observing the tradition of the elders; and when they come from the market place, they do not eat unless they purify themselves; and there are many other traditions which they observe, the washing of cups and pots and vessels of bronze.) And the Pharisees and the scribes asked him, "Why do your disciples not live according to the tradition of the elders, but eat with hands defiled?" And he said to them, "Well did Isaiah prophesy of you hypocrites, as it is written, 'This people honours me with their lips, but their heart is far from me; in vain do they worship me, teaching as doctrines the precepts of men.' You leave the commandment of God, and hold fast the tradition of men." (*Mk* 7:1-8)

Here Jesus undeniably is condemning certain traditions, but it is important to recognise *which* traditions. In this case, they were "precepts of men" that were being put forth by the Pharisees and the scribes as doctrines. They were man-made rules imposed by the Pharisees that put an undue burden on the Jews. The Pharisees had no authority to represent such rules as doctrines. Jesus's rightful condemnation of the Pharisees' practice does not amount to a blanket rejection of the concept of Sacred Tradition.

Another favourite verse of *sola scriptura* adherents is, "See to it that no one makes a prey of you by philosophy and empty deceit, according to human tradition, according to the elemental spirits of the universe, and not according to Christ" (*Col* 2:8). Here, Paul seems to be echoing Jesus's condemnations related by Mark above. Note that it is mere "human tradition" that he denounces. Indeed, the "philosophy" Paul mentions here is likely a reference to man-made precepts of the Jewish law.

Certainly the Catholic Church agrees with Paul that empty and deceitful human traditions are to be rejected. But Sacred Tradition is not such a tradition. It is the teaching of Jesus and the apostles, passed on over time and guided by the Holy Spirit. It is not deceitful but true; it is not human in origin but divine.

It is certainly true that any tradition that contradicts Scripture must be false, because God's revelation cannot contradict itself, but this doesn't make Sacred Tradition inferior to Scripture. For it is *likewise* true that any proposed Scripture or interpretation of Scripture that contradicts Sacred Tradition is false and must be rejected. Scripture must be tested against Tradition to see if it is apostolic.

This was, in fact, one of the ways in which the canon of the New Testament was selected. The Church Fathers who established the canon rejected any texts that contained doctrines contrary to the traditions the apostles had handed down to them.

From texts such as the Gnostic Gospels (for example, the Gospel of Thomas) to Marcion's edited version of Luke's Gospel and Paul's epistles, there were a lot of heretical writings proposed by different groups for inclusion in the New Testament. But the Church determined that they contradicted the Tradition handed down to them from the apostles, and so must have been forged or otherwise non-inspired writings.

Having said all this, it is important to recognise that not *all* man-made traditions are necessarily bad. In addition to Sacred Tradition, Jesus also gave the apostles and their successors the authority to enact practices (which over time become traditions) that are not part of divine revelation but are nonetheless binding on the faithful. Jesus told Peter, "I will give you the keys of the kingdom of heaven, and whatever you bind on earth shall be bound in heaven, and whatever you loose on earth shall be loosed in heaven" (*Mt* 16:19). Later on, Jesus gave similar authority to bind and loose to other apostles gathered together as a unit (see *Mt* 18:18).

The *Catechism* explains that the power to bind and loose "connotes the authority to absolve sins, to pronounce doctrinal judgments, and to make disciplinary decisions in the Church. Jesus entrusted this authority to the Church through the ministry of the apostles and in particular through the ministry of Peter". (*CCC* 553)

Thus, it is necessary first to distinguish between Sacred Tradition and human tradition, always holding fast to the former. It is also necessary to distinguish between human traditions imposed with proper authority and those not, and to give due assent to the former. Although human tradition is inferior to both Sacred Tradition and Sacred Scripture, human traditions may be lawfully enacted - and obeyed - under the Church's authority to bind and loose.

18. Since Jesus commonly quoted Sacred Scripture in his disputes with the Pharisees and the Sadducees, doesn't this prove that he saw the Bible as the sole rule of faith?

Jesus did quote Scripture (the Old Testament) often, but this doesn't prove or even imply that he saw the Bible alone as authoritative. After all: Catholics cite Scripture, too, in support of their views, yet we clearly do not believe the Bible to be the sole rule of faith.

Jesus quoted from the Old Testament because it is the word of God and as such is authoritative for settling the theological questions it addresses. Furthermore, because both Jesus and his opponents accepted Scripture as an authority, he could appeal to it as common ground between them. Here he followed his usual practice of using what his opponents would, in theory at least, accept as binding. But consider his dispute with the Sadducees over the resurrection of the body:

> The same day Sadducees came to him, who say that there is no resurrection; and they asked him a question, saying, "Teacher, Moses said, 'If a man dies, having no children, his brother must marry the widow, and raise up children for his brother.' Now there were seven brothers among us; the first married, and died, and having no children left his wife to his brother. So too the second and third, down to the seventh. After them all, the woman died. In the resurrection, therefore, to which of the seven will she be wife? For they all had her." But Jesus answered them, "You are wrong, because you know neither the scriptures nor the power of God. For in the resurrection they neither marry nor are given in marriage, but are like angels in heaven. And as for the resurrection of the dead, have you not read what was said to you by God, 'I am the God of Abraham, and the God of Isaac, and the God of Jacob'? He is not God of the dead, but of the living." And when the crowd heard it, they were astonished at his teaching. (*Mt* 22:23-33).

The Sadducees, who accepted as inspired only the Pentateuch (the first five books of the Old Testament), didn't believe in the resurrection of the body. In refuting them, Christ *quoted only from the Pentateuch* (*Ex* 3:6), not because he didn't acknowledge other Old Testament books that explicitly mention the resurrection of the body (for example, Daniel), but because the Sadducees didn't accept these other books. An appeal to an authority they didn't accept would have been useless, so Jesus proved his point by referring to one the Sadducees would affirm.

This same type of approach is necessary no matter who a person is challenged by. Sticking to what is recognised as authoritative by both parties will often help to resolve a dispute. But such an approach should not be mistaken as an indication that the authority cited is the sole rule of faith.

19. Doesn't the biblical example of the Bereans prove that Scripture is the true rule of faith and Sacred Tradition is meaningless?

In Acts of the Apostles, Luke briefly tells us about St Paul's missionary work at Berea:

> The brethren immediately sent Paul and Silas away by night to Berea; and when they arrived they went into the Jewish synagogue. Now these Jews were nobler than those in Thessalonica, for they received the word with all eagerness, examining the scriptures daily to see if these things were so. Many of them therefore believed, with not a few Greek women of high standing as well as men. (*Ac* 17:10-12)

Some Protestants latch on to this short passage believing that the example of the Bereans provides evidence for *sola scriptura*. After all, the Bereans examined *Scripture* to test the word, not any tradition. Some imagine the Bereans faithfully living according to what the Bible and the Bible alone taught, until Paul came along claiming to be a teacher. Then they cautiously listened to what he had to say but only went along with it insofar as it agreed with what their Bibles - their sole rule of faith - had to say. Shouldn't today's Christians follow their example?

A closer look at the passage, however, reveals that the people of Berea were not *sola scriptura* adherents at all. Indeed, what Luke commends them for is not their adherence to Scripture alone, but their eagerness in receiving "the word" that Paul delivered to them.

Notice Luke's use of the terms "the word" and "the scriptures." He is talking about two different things here. First, he commends the Bereans for being nobler than the Thessalonians because they eagerly received "the word" (from Paul). What was "the word" they received and what were "the scriptures" they examined?

Luke tells us that the Bereans were mainly Jews (and some Greeks), not Christians, and they even had a Jewish synagogue. The word he took to them was most certainly the gospel message Jesus commissioned him to deliver (see *Ac* 9:15), the same message he sums up in his first letter to the Corinthians: "For I delivered to you as of first importance what I also received, that Christ died for our sins in accordance with the scriptures" (*1 Co* 15:3). "The word" the Bereans received was Paul's oral preaching of the gospel. It was Sacred Tradition! "The scriptures" Paul mentions to the Corinthians are the same scriptures the Bereans examined - the Old Testament that was coming alive in light of Sacred Tradition. That was the only written Scripture recognised in the day.

Thus, what was going on in Berea was the evangelisation of a community primarily made up of Jews whom Paul was teaching about Christianity prior to the existence of the New Testament. The Bereans eagerly listened to Paul bring the Old Testament to life through the teaching he received from Christ, and *this* is what Luke commends them for - their eagerness in receiving Sacred Tradition. As we saw earlier, it is right to use Scripture and Tradition to test each other, and the Bereans provide an example of that by "examining the scriptures" in order to verify that the oral Tradition handed them by Paul was likewise divinely revealed and an authoritative rule of faith.

This all makes sense when we understand the event in its historical context. The event occurred during Paul's second missionary journey. On his journeys Paul taught the good news of Christianity as Jesus had commissioned him to do. As a Jewish convert to Christianity himself, he knew the Old Testament well and he knew that it prophesied about Jesus. In the company of Jews he undoubtedly explained the Old Testament in light of Sacred Tradition in order to show them about the truth of Christianity. They, in turn, would examine the Old Testament and see it come to life.

As a result, many Jews - including many of the Bereans - became Christians.

The Bereans, therefore, do not prove *sola scriptura;* nor did they even practice it themselves. If they did, they never would have "eagerly received" the Tradition that Paul preached.

20. Does the Catholic Church emphasise Sacred Tradition so much that it makes the Bible seem unimportant? Isn't that why the Church historically tried to prevent people from reading it?

These are common misconceptions. The truth is that Catholics meditate on Scripture every day at every Mass. The readings and the responsorial Psalm during the Liturgy of the Word are taken directly from the Bible. The prayers throughout are biblically based. In fact, every moment of the Mass is influenced by Sacred Scripture. But even outside the Mass, the Church teaches that Scripture should always be available to enrich the lives of Catholics as much as possible. *Dei Verbum* exhorts:

> Easy access to Sacred Scripture should be provided for all the Christian faithful. That is why the Church from the very beginning accepted as her own that very ancient Greek translation of the Old Testament which is called the Septuagint; and she has always given a

> place of honour to other Eastern translations and Latin ones especially the Latin translation known as the Vulgate. (*DV* 22)

From its earliest days, the Church has embraced Sacred Scripture and desired to give the faithful access to its richness. That's why St Jerome, who said, "Ignorance of Scripture is ignorance of Christ," translated the Bible into Latin in the fourth century - it was the era's most popular language of the literate.

Dei Verbum goes on to promote the reading of Sacred Scripture in the daily lives of Catholics:

> The sacred synod also earnestly and especially urges all the Christian faithful, especially Religious, to learn by frequent reading of the divine Scriptures the "excellent knowledge of Jesus Christ" (*Ph* 3:8)…Therefore, they should gladly put themselves in touch with the sacred text itself, whether it be through the liturgy, rich in the divine word, or through devotional reading, or through instructions suitable for the purpose and other aids which, in our time, with approval and active support of the shepherds of the Church, are commendably spread everywhere. (*DV* 25)

Clearly, no matter what other people might think, there can be no doubt that the Church wants the faithful to have ready access to Scripture and to make the study of it an ordinary part of Christian life. Dispelling any doubt about how important this is understood to be, the Church even grants indulgences (partial remission of the temporal punishment due for sin) for reading the Bible prayerfully and with reverence.

So what about stories of the Church trying to keep people from reading Scripture by chaining Bibles to churches or burning early printed copies of the Bible?

In the Middle Ages, hand-copied Bibles were sometimes chained up inside churches, but this was to *ensure* access to them, not to deny it. Such books were extremely rare and valuable - not something the average Christian (who was often illiterate, anyway) could buy and keep in his home like he can today - and the only way to give people access to them while at the same time preserving them from theft or damage was to lock them down securely. And what better place to do that than at church, where Christians gathered?

Johann Gutenberg, a German Catholic, is often credited with being the first printer of Bibles. The first book he printed was the Mazarin Bible, so called because a copy was discovered in Cardinal Jules Mazarin's library. It is more commonly known today as the Gutenberg Bible and it was printed more than sixty years before the advent of Protestantism. So the Church did not oppose the printing of Bibles, or, later, the translation of Bibles into vernacular languages.

Even so, very poor, even heretical, translations of the Bible have surfaced from time to time, and these can be a danger to anyone who is not aware of the problematic content they contain. In order to protect unwary faithful from studying them, the Church has condemned and even destroyed erroneous translations. Far from downplaying the importance of Scripture, the Church's vigilant concern for the integrity of God's written word demonstrates the great value it has historically placed on it.

Today, with widespread printing and even electronic editions of Bibles, the Church can't possibly monitor every translation that pops up. The Church does, however, offer guidelines for the benefit of the faithful: encouraging "suitable and correct translations" to ensure that Sacred Scripture "be accessible at all times," and charging bishops with the solemnly important task of instructing their flock in the "right use" of Scripture, "so that the children of the Church may safely and profitably become conversant with the Sacred Scriptures and be penetrated with their spirit" (*DV* 22).

Endnotes

[1] See Hebrews 11:3, Revelation 19:3.

[2] J.N.D. Kelly, *Early Christian Doctrines* (New York, Harper Collins, 1978) 53.

[3] Yves Congar, OP, *The Meaning of Tradition* (San Francisco, Ignatius Press, 2004), p. 22.

[4] *Against Heresies* 1:10:2.

[5] Ibid. 3:3:1.

[6] *The Fundamental Doctrines* 1:2.

[7] Fragment in Eusebius, *Church History* 3:39.

[8] Ibid. 4:21.

[9] *On Baptism, Against the Donatists* 5:23.

[10] Ibid. 5:26.

[11] *Responsum ad Dubium on Ordinatio Sacerdotalis* (1995).

[12] Most of the Eastern Catholic churches, in full communion with the Catholic Church, do ordain married men in keeping with their historical practice. And even in the Western (Roman-rite) church, in some circumstances married men - for example, converts who had been previously ordained in another Christian church - may likewise be ordained.

[13] *Address of His Holiness Benedict XVI to the Roman Curia Offering Them His Christmas Greetings* (2005).

[14] For example, see Justin Martyr, *First Apology* 61; Irenaeus, *Fragment* 34; Tertullian, *Baptism* 12:1; Augustine, *The City of God* 13:7; etc.

[15] For example, in 1 Corinthians 7:32-34, St. Paul notes how those who are unmarried (like himself) are better able to devote themselves to God.

[16] *Catholic Encyclopedia*, s.vv. "Canon of the Old Testament."

[17] See Acts 2:42; 15:2.

[18] *Letters*, 75:3.

[19] *The Holy Spirit*, 27:66.

[20] *Medicine Chest Against All Heresies*, 61:6.

[21] *Homilies on Second Thessalonians*.

[22] *The Notebooks*.

20 Answers: The Real Jesus

Trent Horn

Who was Jesus? Did he really exist? This booklet provides intelligent responses to the most fundamental questions about Jesus's life, death and resurrection. Topics covered include the veracity of the Gospel accounts, the relationship between Christian religion and pagan mythology and how best to treat the apocryphal gospels and the divinity of Christ.

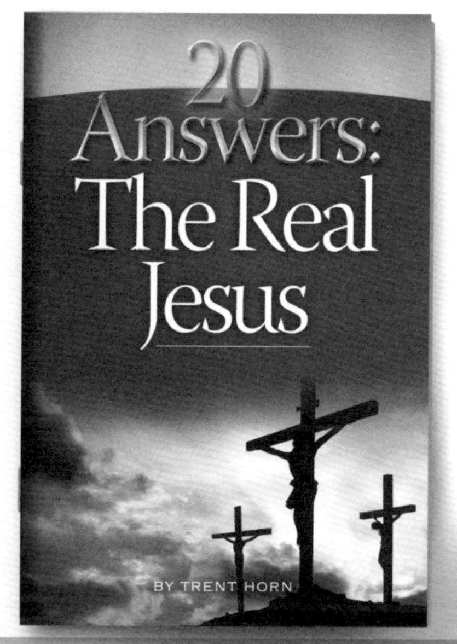

C292 ISBN 978 1 78469 048 9